DOMINICAN DOLL,
CARIBBEAN TREASURE

Muñeca Dominicana,
Caribeño Tesoro

Margarita Suero-Duran

Illustrations by Kenn Yapsangco

ISBN: Softcover   978-1-4931-9570-1
       EBook   978-1-4931-9571-8

Rev. date: 04/29/2014

To order additional copies of this book, contact:
Xlibris LLC
1-888-795-4274
www.Xlibris.com
Orders@Xlibris.com

Para

Mi familia

With a special dedication to

Ariana, Julius, and Melanie

May we honor our heritage, always.

No olvidemos nunca…

Love, *Abuela*

Dominican Doll travels the world with dignity and grace.

Muñeca Dominicana, por el mundo viaja. Digna y con gracia, la verás.

Do you know why she has no face?

¿Por qué no tiene rostro? ¿Lo sabrás?

Dominican Doll is a Caribbean treasure.

Muñeca Dominicana es un Caribeño tesoro.

5

Why faceless? Might you know?

¿Por qué no tiene rostro? ¿Lo sabrás, acaso?

She is made of clay from Antillean soil,

Está hecha de barro del suelo Antillano,

the very same clay from *Taínos* of long ago.

el mismo barro aquel de los Taínos del ayer.

11

Her *Taíno* legacy,
she will never forget.

*Su legado Taíno,
no lo olvidará jamás.*

Why faceless? Would anyone know?

¿Por qué no tiene rostro? ¿Quién lo ha de saber?

Faceless, she embraces her humble roots,

Sin rostro, reconoce sus humildes raíces,

**Knowing where she came from
and dreaming of where she might go.**

*Recordando de donde viene
y soñando hacia donde ir.*

15

Her heritage is _Taíno_,

Su herencia es Taína,

16

European,

Europea,

and African.

y Africana.

Why faceless? She wants us to know.

¿Por qué no tiene rostro? Ella nos quiere decir.

Faceless, she embraces the diversity of her roots.

Sin rostro, representa la diversidad de sus raíces.

**Born in *Quisqueya*,
she is honored to show...**

*Ha nacido en Quisqueya
con orgullo profundo.*

21

Caribbean pride in a blended heritage...

Caribeño tesoro de herencias unidas,

reflecting cultures of the world wherever she may go.

en ella se reflejan las culturas del mundo.

Printed in the United States
by Baker & Taylor Publisher Services